Zen and Now

Dreama Denver
illustrated by Jan Philpot

Headline Books
Terra Alta, WV

Zen and Now

by Dreama Denver

illustrated by Jan Philpot

copyright ©2022 Dreama Denver

To order additional copies of this book or for book publishing information, or to contact the author:

Headline Books
P.O. Box 52
Terra Alta, WV 26764
www.HeadlineBooks.com

Tel: 304-789-3001
Email: mybook@headlinebooks.com

ISBN 13: 9781951556860

Library of Congress Control Number: 2022934713

PRINTED IN THE UNITED STATES OF AMERICA

To the forgotten, abandoned, unwanted animals waiting in shelters all over the world, and to the humans who make the choice to take them home and rewrite their future. Thank you! This faithful companion will love you to the last beat of his heart.

TABLE OF CONTENT

1

There she was, walking toward me, her eyes looking straight into mine. My little heart was pounding because I saw something in her eyes that told me **this** was my person. To me, she was beautiful, all golden, with her blonde hair and her 100-megawatt smile. As she got closer, I picked up her scent and knew it was a scent I'd remember all the days of my life. I felt myself wanting to squirm from the tip of my nose all the way to my toes. My tail was thumping against the crate in my excitement. Then I heard her voice.

"Will it be okay if I take him out of the crate and walk him around for a while?"

Suddenly a leash appeared, the crate door opened, and just like that, I was stepping out into the sunlight with the leash around my neck. I blinked as this angel (I don't know what else to call her) stooped down to my level and caressed my face with her hand. *Okay, I told myself, Sit here quietly. Be the picture of the perfect dog.* And even though every part of me wanted to

run around in endless circles, even though I had this undeniable urge to lick her all over her face as a way of telling her what I couldn't say in words, I sat as quietly as I could while she looked me over.

"Hey there, buddy," she whispered as she stroked my face. "Wow! You are one handsome boy! How is it you haven't been adopted?"

Because I've been waiting for you, I wanted to shout. You're my person, I know it and I've been waiting for you!

"Soooo," she continued, "do you think we'd get along?"

Would we get along? Of course, we'd get along! I'd make sure of it.

"Do you think you might like to come home with me?"

She had to be kidding, right? But she continued, deep in thought, "You're a big dog, but I love big dogs...I have a fairly big house with plenty of room for you...and my property would be perfect, on top of a mountain, surrounded by woods, a couple of ponds...plenty of room for you to run and explore."

Oh, my goodness! God was looking out for me by sending an angel to rescue me! But before my doggie brain could come up with a way to thank God properly, she flashed her big, golden smile at me.

"I'll tell you what, let's walk around for a bit and get to know each other a little better." I stood at attention as she ran her hands up and down my back. I know you don't get a second chance to make a first impression, so I wanted to be on my best behavior. I wanted her to like me...no, I wanted her to *LOVE* me!

When I was a tiny puppy, I had a different name, but I can't really remember what it was all these years later. You see, when I was a year old, I was rescued by my person, who, as it ended up, needed me as much as I needed her. I think it's pretty safe to say we rescued each other. I needed to be rescued because I was found roaming the streets of a small town. No one knew why I was out there all by myself. Of course, I knew why, but as a dog with no command of the English language,

I couldn't explain, but I can tell you now, it was pretty scary and lonely not having a nice warm place to sleep and someone to love me. When I was found alone and scared, I was taken to the local animal shelter. After being there for about a month, I heard a couple of the staff members talking about the fact I hadn't been adopted yet. "We'll give it a couple more days and then he'll have to be euthanized," I heard one say. I had no idea what that word meant, but judging by the reaction of the other dogs, I knew it couldn't be good.

One day passed and I could feel myself becoming anxious. *Hadn't they said something about a couple of days? What would happen to me after a couple of days?* Hunkering down in my cage, I curled up to calm myself down. *Breathe*, I told myself, *it's all going to be okay.* I wasn't sure if I believed me, but I had to try to find some peace in this strange circumstance. Downward dog hadn't worked, so I'm guessing that only worked for humans. Finally, I managed to doze off and settled into nice REM sleep when I heard voices. Humans! Heading my way! I sat straight up to look them directly in the eye when they got to my cage.

Two ladies stared down at me. They said they were from an animal rescue organization. Crouching down to my eye level, the rescue lady looked me over and asked a few questions, which the shelter human hurried to answer.

"Well, he's a Husky/Shepherd mix. We think probably a year old, maybe a little older. He was found roaming the streets alone, which none of us can understand, given how handsome he is. He should have been put to sleep already, but we just haven't been able to bring ourselves to do it; however, we're now out of time, and it's scheduled for tomorrow."

"No, no, that can't happen," the rescue lady insisted. "We'll find him a foster family and then a forever home. That's that! He's leaving with us."

And that's how my life was saved, and I ended up in foster care, dreaming about my person and the beautiful life I was sure we could have together.

My person, who I think of as my human mom, had gone through some recent losses too, which meant she was living alone in a great big house exactly like the one I'd been dreaming of. You know the kind – two stories with lots of room to explore and a variety of places where I could catch a catnap anytime I felt like it, a nice leather sofa with a spot at the end exactly the right size for me and a yard so big I could take off running at top speed and run for a full minute without stopping. But I digress. This story isn't just *my* story; it's *our* story and I want to give Mom a chance to tell you what our first meeting was like for her.

2

Filled with excitement, I practically danced toward the crate as I made my way through the throng of people. I came here in search of a new best friend. It was Friday night, and at the local high school football game, an animal rescue organization was there hoping to find forever homes for some very deserving dogs. I, as it happened, needed a new best friend to share my life with me. You see, for the first time in my life, I was alone. I suppose being alone wasn't necessarily all bad, but I had tried it and, quite honestly, wasn't all that fond of it, so the search was on. For some reason, I had a very good feeling about tonight.

As I approached the crate, I honestly couldn't believe what I saw. Without a doubt, this was one of the most gorgeous dogs I had ever seen. Big brown eyes stared at me from his all-white face and his ears stood straight up. Shades of black and gray covered his back and much of his long, fluffy tail. As I got closer, I could see the long white eyelashes framing his soulful brown eyes. If eyes are the windows to the soul, and I believe they are, then this beautiful boy was as soulful as they come. Someone I loved very much years before had given me this solid advice, *when choosing a rescue, look deep into the eyes to connect with the animal's soul.* Our eyes locked and our souls collided with a connection so deep I knew I had found my best friend. His tail thumped against the floor of the crate and I knew he felt it too.

"Will it be okay if I take him out of the crate and walk him around for a while?" I asked my friend Kathy, who was part of the rescue organization. Leash in hand, she opened the crate and set him free. He stepped out into the sunlight, blinking. Then he looked me square in the eye. Be still my heart! He was gorgeous and so well-behaved! I stooped down to caress his face. "Hey there, buddy," I whispered as I stroked his face. "Wow! You are one handsome boy! How is it you haven't been adopted?" But deep in my heart, I knew the answer to my question*: because he was meant for me. This was* my *dog, my destiny. The two of us were meant to be! It was as simple as that!*

"Soooo, do you think we'd get along? (thump, thump) Do you think you might like to come home with me? (thump, thump) You're a big dog, but I love big dogs...and I have a big house with plenty of room for you...and my property would be perfect. It's on top of a mountain, surrounded by woods, a couple of ponds... plenty of room for you to run and explore." Something

told me he liked the idea because even though he was on his best behavior, his tail thumped furiously, and I could tell he wanted to run, jump, let go and be a dog. "I tell you what, let's walk around for a bit and get to know each other a little better." And that's what we did. I led him away from all the other people and we walked quietly together. Kathy had given me dog treats to share with him, so I'd tell him to sit, which amazingly he did perfectly with no training from me, and when he did, I'd reward him with a treat. We found a little bench where I sat down, looked him in the eye, and told him my circumstances, why I needed him so much. The understanding I saw in his eyes was almost human. I had a feeling he knew *precisely* what I meant.

After a while, Kathy came over to sit with us, telling me what her rescue organization knew about his history – found alone roaming the streets, a male Husky/Shepherd mix, possibly a year old, maybe slightly older, now with a foster family, but had been at the animal shelter where he was one day away from being put to sleep. After that last sentence, her words became white noise in my head as I tried to wrap my mind around how close this beautiful boy had come to not being here for me to meet. It was unimaginable! I loved rescues. During my lifetime, I have rescued many dogs and many cats. And each one had been unique and different; each one had brought a special joy into my life, but animals have a much shorter life span than humans, so now I was alone again, and my house felt empty with just me in it.

So, here I was on a Friday night, looking for a new best friend. Yes, I wanted to rescue a dog who needed me as well as the home I could provide. Still, the truth was, I needed to be rescued too – rescued from the solitary life I was living, rescued from lonely nights sitting in front of the television with no one to talk to, rescued from the emptiness of having no one to love and care for. As I walked around with this handsome fella, I knew he was the one. How did I know? I knew by the way he looked at me with those big brown eyes. I knew by the instant connection I felt with him. I knew because I had prayed to find a beautiful boy just like this one and God had answered my prayers. God knew. He knew days were coming when the two of us would need each other. He knew the comfort we would bring each other. He knew the pure joy we would find in each other's company. He knew...and I'm thankful every day that His plan for my life included the handsome fella on the other end of this red leash. Yes, this was the dog for me! God knew, and now, so did I.

3

COMING HOME

The adoption papers were signed. The adoption fees were paid. My foster family loaded me into a crate in the back of their truck and we were off! From everything I'd heard them say, I was pretty sure we were heading to my forever home. Being a dog, especially a dog in the back of a truck, not knowing exactly where you're going, is a strange feeling, but deep in my doggie heart, I hoped they were taking me to the special lady I had met a couple of days before. *Had it only been a couple of days?* It felt like I had been dreaming about her for much longer than a few days. I remembered her smile, her voice and her scent. I will never forget her scent. Something told me if I picked up her scent again, I would be safe and loved forever.

By the motion in the back of the truck, I could tell we were going up a mountain. *Hadn't she told me she lived on top of a mountain? Yes, I'm sure that's what she had said.* Even though I was lying down, the mountain curves had me swaying in my crate. After a few minutes, we stopped going up and leveled out. Did this mean we were at the top of the mountain? *Did this mean she was close by?* I pushed my nose up against the bars of the crate. If she was anywhere nearby, my 200 million scent receptors should be able to smell her even from a mile away. I sniffed. I sniffed again. Wait! There it was! Her scent! I was picking up her scent! Dogs often associate scents with positive memories and my recollections of her were my best memories ever. Her scent must mean we were getting close to my forever home. Please, please, please let that be true!

The truck made a left then came to a stop. Her scent was strong now and every part of me started quivering. My tail was thumping hard against the crate's floor. I was panting with excitement. The truck's tailgate was lowered, revealing my foster mom, who smiled at me and assured me I was finally HOME! And suddenly, like a dream come true, the special lady walked into my line of sight – still golden, still angelic, and from this moment forward, all mine. My person, my human, my master...my mom. Not only did I have a forever home, but now I had a forever mom. To the person reading this book – think about your mom, how much she loves you, how she makes you feel safe, how you're the most important thing in her life. Isn't that the best feeling? Well, now I had that feeling too because today

I finally had a mom of my very own. And starting right this second, that's how I would think of her...my mom.

My foster mom opened the crate and I jumped out of the back of the truck. There, right in front of me, stood my new mom. She had a huge smile on her face. "Hey there, buddy," she started toward me, "welcome home!" I couldn't stop myself. I tried, but my legs had a mind of their own. Before I could stop myself, I ran the fifteen feet that separated us, and then before my brain could tell my feet NO, I had my two front paws on her shoulders and my face level with hers. We were nose-to-nose, eyeball-to-eyeball. Her look of surprise turned into the look of love as she kissed the tip of my nose. "You have no idea how happy I am to have you here with me," she said as she scratched my ears. "My beautiful boy!" My tongue literally was hanging out of my mouth in ecstasy. This had to be the earthly version of heaven. I was home with my new mom. She gave my foster mom a quick hug, thanking her over and over, then turned to me as the truck pulled out of the driveway.

"So, what do you think?" she asked matter-of-factly. *What did I think? Looking around, I couldn't help but wonder if this was all a great big, beautiful dream. Everything about my new home was perfect! There was a huge yard, trees everywhere, a pond I could drink from if I got thirsty, a shaded front porch where I could get out of the sun when I felt too hot, and, best of all; there was Mom.*

"I've spent all weekend trying to decide what to name you. You're a very special dog, so it can't be just any old name." She sat down in the grass, patting the ground next to her, inviting me to sit down beside her. I did. Gazing off into the mountains in the distance, she continued to scratch behind my ears as she spoke, "My life has been anything but peaceful in the last few years. We don't need to go into all the details, but the bottom line is, I've been alone."

I nuzzled her hand. *Boy, did I know what being alone felt like. I never wanted to feel those feelings again.* She kept talking as she continued to scratch my ears, "And being alone so much of the time with no one to talk to has made me feel sad, but...the sadness ends today because now, I have you. Whatever happens, we'll go through it together. It'll be you and me against the world. Whatever happens, I'll be there for you, and you'll be there for me. Best buddies always, okay?" I laid my head in her lap as a way to answer, yes!

"I've needed some Zen in my life," she continued with a faraway look in her eyes. "When life throws us curves when unexpected things happen, I think we humans long for peace and calm. That's what the word Zen means – peace, calm, oneness – and that's what I felt the minute we saw each other, a sense of peacefulness, a sense that we belonged together." A huge smile covered her face, "And I'm happy to say talking to you like this, loving on you like this, spending time with you like this makes me feel calm. You fill the bill in every way, my friend." She jumped to her feet and I jumped to mine. Spreading her arms wide, she spun in a circle, laughing, "Welcome to the top of the mountain, sweet boy. All of this is yours to explore. I'm so happy to have you in my life! Welcome HOME, Zen!

ZEN! That was my new name! I liked it. No, I *loved* it! My doggie heart was ready to burst. I had gone from being nameless and walking the streets alone to living on this beautiful mountaintop with the angel who rescued me. And, as she would remind me many times during our years together, unknowingly, I had also rescued her. That statement filled me with joy and made me feel like a superhero. The two of us really had saved each other and the bond between us could never be broken. We both knew as long as we had each other, we would never be alone again.

4

LEARNING THE DOS AND DON'TS

Mom and I were settling into a routine. Well, let's put it this way, I was working hard to learn the routine, all the dos and don'ts. I wanted nothing more than to please her, so I paid very close attention when she corrected me. And the best part was, she never yelled at me; only told me gently what was acceptable and what wasn't. For example, the first time I walked into her living room, I saw a wooden table. Hey, it was wood, so as far as I knew, it was fair game. I lifted my leg, but before I could mark it (because you know that's what we male dogs do – we make it our business to mark everything), she looked down at me and said something like, *no, no, no, we never lift our leg inside the house!* Good to know! I never lifted my leg inside the house again.

Then there was the time we were in the kitchen together. I forget exactly what she was doing, but I knew for sure I wanted to be part of it. I nonchalantly moved over right next to her and placed my front paws on the kitchen counter. Let me tell you how exciting that was. First, I could see *everything* from this high up. There was something she called a sink and any time she wanted, she could turn on this shiny silver thing and the sink would fill up with water!! There was something else she called a cooktop and the weird thing was when she turned a knob on this cooktop thing, there were circles that got really red and very hot. I knew this because my paws were close enough to feel some of the heat. Even I knew this was too close for comfort, so when Mom turned back to me and saw that we were eye to eye because my paws were on the counter making me as tall as she was, she gently took both paws in her hands and placed them back on the floor where they belonged, saying, "Zen, it's my job to keep you safe and counter surfing isn't safe." *So that's what it was called – counter surfing!*

"Your back legs could slip on the wood floor and you could fall and hurt yourself." – *wow, I never thought of that* – "You could burn your front paws on the cooktop." – *yep, that thought had definitely occurred to me* – "If I forget and leave something like chocolate on the kitchen counter and you eat it, you could get very sick." – *It's true. I loved to eat and if I was hungry enough, I'd eat just about anything* – "Remember how we talked about taking care of each other? Well, sweet boy, this is me looking out for you." *Kids, when someone cares about you enough to keep you from harm's way, that's a sure sign you are loved. Don't forget that!*

Our first days together we did nothing but explore – just the two of us, getting to know each other, falling in love - and there was so much to discover on top of the mountain. First, I made it my mission to mark every tree, every bush, basically every blade of grass I could find. That took a lot of pee, let me tell you, but, as I said, it's what we male dogs do. It's called marking our territory.

There was lots of wildlife on the mountain and I wanted to make sure they knew this particular part of the mountain belonged to *me*. During our walks, Mom and I saw rabbits, wild turkeys, beautiful, elegant deer families, and once, we even saw a bear cub way off in the distance. I remember the first time we walked out the front door and saw five deer in our driveway. Right there in our driveway!! We both stopped short as the deer lifted their heads and stared at us. I could feel myself wanting to run for them, mainly to play with them. *Hmmmm*, I wondered, *which one would be the best playmate if they scattered in all directions and I had to chase just one?* Hoping for some direction, I tilted my head to look up at Mom just as she looked down at me. "I see it in your eyes and I know it's your nature, but let's just enjoy the deer from a distance, okay? That way, they'll visit us more often." And that's exactly what we did, and the best part was, the deer visited almost on a daily basis.

The most important thing in my life was pleasing my mom. After all, she had rescued me, given me a safe place to live and all the food I needed. She loved on me, cuddled with me and made me feel like the luckiest dog in the world. So, I tried to come up with little ways to show my love for her. This may sound silly, but one of my habits that most impressed her revolved around doing #2. You know what I mean by #2, right? Like I've mentioned before, I would pee on everything in sight, but #2 was another matter. I looked around at her well-kept yard and knew I didn't want to leave something smelly behind for her to step in accidentally and track through our beautiful house. So...the first time we went outside for me to do my business, I surveyed the property. Since I was pretty smart, it didn't take me long to hone in on the upper yard that bordered the woods. *Perfect*, I thought to myself, *if I did my business right there on the edge of the woods, far away from the house, there's no way she would ever step in it.* What I didn't expect was her reaction after I had done this a few times. Boy, did she love me! We rolled in the grass far away from the woods; she hugged me, called me her 'good boy,' told me I was undoubtedly the smartest dog she had ever met, then took me inside and gave me treats. I just grinned at her. Yep, I knew how to grin and I have pictures to prove it.

There was no doubt about it. I was livin' the life on top of the hill and doing my business at the edge of the woods.

5

Shopping, Drive-thrus, and Banking

Wanna know something cool? My mom owns a radio station. Wanna hear something even cooler? Her radio station was in our house, upstairs to be exact. I don't know how many dogs get to go to work with their person every day, but I did!

Every morning while it was still dark, she would get up, brush her teeth, wash her face, and off we'd go up the stairs to work. I have to admit it was pretty cool, even if I didn't quite understand it all. At 7:00 in the morning, she'd open the mics and welcome her listeners to the show she called "Sunny Side Up." I loved the name of the show because it sounded happy. She and her co-host Steve would start talking practically nonstop to people who weren't actually there in the room with us, and they did this for THREE hours! They also played music, which I really liked because almost every time they stopped talking and went back to music Mom would turn around to talk to and love on me. Steve too. Yep, every weekday morning, I got a double dose of love and attention.

During the morning show, I would lie right behind Mom while she talked to the people I couldn't see. I almost never barked. Nope, I wasn't a barking dog, but every once in a while, Mom would give me the signal to speak and, of course, to please her, I did. Her audience loved it and that's when I became one of the most popular features of "Sunny Side Up!" Mom called me her radio star and even though I had no idea exactly what that meant, I could tell by her tone and the love on her face when she said it, being her radio star was a very good thing!

One other thing I remember distinctly about the show was learning to tell time. Let me explain – we dogs don't understand the concept of time in minutes or hours like humans do, but we do have a *sense* of time. We can anticipate future events based on past experience, so after a few months of Mom and Steve taking me for a short walk at a certain point during the show, I came to anticipate the 9 o'clock hour. When my sense told me it was time for our walk, I'd stand up, squiggle my way over to her and either poke her with my nose or lay my head in her lap. I can't tell you how excited this made her, convincing her I was the smartest dog on the face of the earth. "Would you look at this," she'd say to the audience, "how does my boy know exactly when it's time for his walk?!?" I had to grin. Being a radio star definitely had its perks!

The first time Mom told me we were going shopping, I had no idea what she meant, but, wow, was it fun! If you guys go shopping with your moms, you know exactly what I mean. Sometimes you get a special toy, once in a while you get something yummy to eat, but always you get to be with your favorite person. Because I was a dog, there were places that wouldn't allow me in, which never made sense to us since I am a really good dog, but then there were places that welcomed me with open arms and loved to see me coming. I had two favorites – our local hardware store, which was huge and had smells galore, and our local bank, where the tellers loved me and constantly gave me yummy treats. Remember earlier when I talked about learning the dos and don'ts? Well, shopping trips had a whole new set of dos and don'ts and I learned one of the biggest don'ts the first time Mom and I went to the hardware store.

It was our first Christmas together. Mom was shopping for decorations and a Christmas tree, which is how we ended up in the hardware store in the middle of their Christmas display. I looked around in wonder. There were trees everywhere! The fact they were strung with lights didn't really faze me. I just saw trees, lots and lots of trees with lots and lots of branches and, of course, you know what that meant, don't you? A whole new territory to mark! Even though I was on my leash,

Mom was busy oooh-ing and ahhh-ing over the pretty displays and wasn't really paying close attention. And that's when I did what male dogs do – I lifted my leg and...well, you can guess the rest.

I saw the look on Mom's face when she looked down and saw the puddle I had made and thought to myself, *uh-oh, now I'm in trouble*, but much to my surprise, she started laughing. She laughed so hard tears started down her face, making me wonder if she was laughing the way it seemed or possibly crying. Humans are funny animals.

With no hesitation, she walked me over to the clerk and laughingly told her, "It seems my dog just picked out our new Christmas tree, the one with the puddle underneath. I am so sorry for the inconvenience, but this is his first time shopping, and apparently, he didn't know a real tree from a fake one. If you give me a mop, I'll be glad to clean this up."

The clerk, a really nice lady, looked at me adoringly and scratched my head, "Oh my goodness, he's so handsome. Believe me, this isn't the first time this has happened. We'll take care of it. No worries."

"I can't thank you enough. We'll take it! That very one if it's okay to take the display tree."

Under the circumstances, it must have been perfectly okay because the nice lady called a man over to carry the tree out for us. As we were heading out the door, Mom couldn't help but laugh when she heard over the loudspeaker, *Clean-up in aisle two of holiday displays.*

"Zen, you sure know how to make an impression," she said as she winked at me. I walked out with my head held high. You bet I did!

We left the hardware store and headed straight to the bank, which over the years became one of my favorite places. I got the hang of the drive-thru right away. Mom would pull up to the bank's window and I would stand up in the back seat, tilting my head to one side as I looked straight into the teller's eyes. The minute she spotted me, her eyes would light up and her hand would reach over to her right. The drive-thru drawer would come out and in it would be...not one treat...not two treats...but a whole handful of milk bones just for me!! Is it any wonder I loved the drive-thru? Actually, I loved any drive-thru because the result was always the same – me sitting in the backseat with a smorgasbord of treats coming at me as Mom handed them over her seat.

As good as it was to stay in the car and get treats, it was even better when Mom took me inside the bank. Talk about giddy! The ladies went crazy over me, lining up to pet me, talking sweet talk to me, and yes, giving me treats galore. And since the tellers encouraged it, I was allowed to place my paws on the teller's window and stand up until we were nose-to-nose. Before I did this, I always looked into Mom's eyes for an okay. Did you know dogs are the only non-primate animal to do that? Other animals make eye contact, but a dog's 'need to please' causes us to look into our human's eyes for direction. When her eyes gave me the okay, I lifted up and 'talked' to the teller; at least my version of talking, which came out more like a howl. I can't tell you how badly I wanted to talk like a human, but I'm a dog and can't form words. However, I could definitely do short howls and longer howls to get my point across. The ladies responded with, "Good boy! Oh, my goodness, he's so adorable. Keep talking, Zen. That's it!" I obliged by 'talking' nonstop for what felt like hours.

So, *this* was what it was like to make a personal appearance! Talking up a storm, laying on the charm and doing whatever it took to keep your audience happy. Let me tell you, that's work and can take a lot out of a guy. By the time Mom and I left the bank and got to the car, that back seat was looking pretty good, so I jumped in, plopped down, stretched out, and snoozed all the way home.

6

NURSING HOME VISITS

Life continued on top of the mountain, with Mom and me exploring every nook and cranny of our property. We did our morning show thing, our shopping thing, and our cuddle-up-for-couch-time thing, which meant we had settled into a nice routine. I realized she was part of my pack the night she got down on the floor and spooned with me while we watched television. Getting belly rubs and hearing her voice whisper sweet things in my ear made those some of my favorite times. However, I think I unintentionally hurt her feelings when I wouldn't sleep in her bedroom at night. With tears in her eyes, she said to me, "Buddy, I've never had a dog who didn't sleep right next to the bed. I just don't understand why you won't do that."

How could I explain? I knew she was alone, but all of my senses told me to sleep near the front door, under the stairs, to be exact, just in case there was ever trouble. What kind of trouble? I have no idea. It was just my instinct to protect her, and under the stairs, I could keep tabs on the whole house. Plus, my keen sense of smell and sensitive hearing made it possible for me to know when raccoons or possums came out at night, and, I ask you, who could sleep with all of that nightlife happening right under his nose? After a few months, she finally accepted it, thank goodness. I never wanted to hurt her feelings, but a dog's gotta do what a dog's gotta do.

One day after our morning walk, Mom sat down with me, "Zen, there's someone new I want you to meet." *Great! I loved meeting new people*! "She's a beautiful older lady named Ruby and she lives in a nursing home. Miss Ruby is someone I love and she's very important to me. So, here's what you need to know. Lots of older folks live in nursing homes and many of them don't see their families very often. Many of them have had to leave their dogs and cats behind, which sometimes makes them feel sad and lonely. When we get to the nursing home, you have to be on your best behavior. No barking, no lifting your leg on anything inside and no running. You'll have to be on a leash and right beside me at all times." *Heck, except for the leash, I didn't see a problem and a leash I could handle if I had to. I started spinning in circles, rarin' to go!*

Even though I didn't know what to expect, I was pleasantly surprised when we got there and was welcomed with open arms. The nurses and staff members made a fuss over me, which made me feel good. They took us into a room that was almost all glass, a bright, happy room. Some of the residents were playing a game called BINGO. I know that because every once in a while, someone would yell out, *BINGO,* and everyone would cheer! Some of the residents were watching TV, an old western called "The Virginian," which they remembered from their younger days. Some residents were sitting around a table doing puzzles with their friends and family. You guys know how much fun puzzles can be. Well, it seems they're fun when you're older, too. Mom smiled and talked to some of the folks while we waited for the staff to bring Miss Ruby in. When I first saw her, she was sitting in a chair with wheels, appropriately called a wheelchair, and Mom took over the minute she saw her, rolling her chair over to the huge window where we could see the mountains.

"Miss Ruby, I want you to meet my new best friend, Zen." I sat up straighter. Miss Ruby reached out to touch me. I leaned in to make it easier for her. I looked into Mom's eyes for direction and could tell she approved, so I moved a little closer. Miss Ruby's hands were older, wrinkled, but oh, so soft. She touched me tentatively at first, but as she spoke to me in her soft voice and understood that I was well-behaved and wouldn't snap or snarl or even lick, she buried her fingers in my fur and repeated my name over and over again. Mom told me later that Miss Ruby repeated Zen over and over as a way to remember my name because sometimes older folks have memory problems. That was fine with me. I loved my name. As an equal-opportunity lover, I didn't hesitate to put my muzzle on her knee to give her some unconditional love. Everything about her brightened as she petted me. Her voice got stronger, her attention more focused, she sat up straighter in her wheelchair, all of which seemed to make Mom really happy. And making Mom happy was my most important job.

We sat together for hours and what I loved most about our time was the laughter. Mom and Miss Ruby shared memories, things I knew nothing about, but enjoyed hearing anyway as I lay on the floor next to the wheelchair. They harmonized, singing favorite songs, told stories from long ago, and laughed endlessly. Being able to make Miss Ruby laugh meant the world to Mom, I could tell. Then Mom did something I had seen her do hundreds of times on her morning show. She started asking questions, like an interview. Of course, this time, I could actually *see* the person answering the questions. Suddenly, as if it had just occurred to her, Mom pulled out her iPhone and began recording Miss Ruby's answers. Some of the answers brought tears to both their eyes; some answers caused more laughter. I was happy to just lie there and soak up all the good feelings that surrounded us. The staff was keeping an eye on us, so it wasn't a total surprise when one of them walked over, but her question was a big surprise.

"We've been watching Zen," she said, "and can't believe what a good dog he is. It's amazing how Miss Ruby has responded to him. Would it be possible for him to visit some of the other patients while you're here? Would you have time? So many of our residents miss their pets and we feel Zen would be a huge comfort to them." I may not know much in human terms, but I sensed this was an important job they were asking me to do.

"Oh my gosh! Zen and I would love that, wouldn't we, Zen?" I stood up in answer to her question, ready to go. Whatever they needed, I was prepared! After making sure Miss Ruby knew we'd be right back, we left the glass room and headed down the hall. There were many, many doors up and down the hallway and behind every single door was someone who lived in the nursing home. Mom and I went from room to room. I'm a big dog, have I mentioned that before? I think I have. Well, being a big dog was working in my favor today because I was tall enough for most of the residents to reach me easily. Some of them threw their arms wide open and begged me to lay my head on their bed so they could pet me, which, of course, I did happily. Some of them were a little hesitant, but after checking with Mom, I put them at ease by giving them a very gentle lick to let them know they were safe with me. I got called lots of different names that day – Sophie, Gracie, Pippin, Scout, Piper, Mr. Moto, Shaba, and even Priss, but Mom explained to me that when they petted me, these folks were remembering the dogs and cats they had left behind and, in their hearts, they were petting them. That was a-okay with me. I would answer to any name they wanted to call me. And that's the day I became an unofficial therapy dog, and as good as I made these folks feel, they made me feel even better. Mom, too. We were welcomed at the nursing home anytime, so Mom and I went often and both of us felt all the better for it every time we visited.

I want to share this with you because I think it's important. There is so much to be learned from the older people in our lives. They have so much wisdom, have lived through decades of history, and have endless love to give. I know because Miss Ruby and the other residents at the nursing home loved me big time! Spending time with me eased their loneliness and lifted their spirits, so just imagine what seeing a grandchild or a great-grandchild could do. You exist because they exist, so it's only right to make sure they know they're loved. I exist because Mom rescued me and Mom exists because Miss Ruby lived. Yes, as time went by, I came to understand that Miss Ruby was her mother and without Miss Ruby in this world, I wouldn't have my lovely home or my beautiful person. And, of course, the fact they were mother and daughter meant I was Miss Ruby's granddog. I was a granddog! And that made me adore her all the more.

7

ADAM NAMES THE CREATURES

It was couch-cuddle time, my very favorite time of the day. Mom invited me to jump up on the sofa, which I did joyfully, settling into the crook of her arm. She hugged me up. I loved couch cuddle time because she always told me stories. Sometimes they were stories about her life. Sometimes they were stories that made her cry, giving me the chance to love on her and make her feel better. Sometimes they were stories about me and how smart I was, how funny I was, how much she loved me and how the two of us had saved each other. I loved when she told me the story of how we met and how much she loved me the minute we laid eyes on each other. I couldn't talk, which made it impossible to tell her I felt the same way about the two of us and our first meeting, so I did the next best thing. I gently licked her hand and snuggled in closer. Her kiss on top of my head told me she understood.

"Zen," she said to me, "today I'm going to tell you an amazing story I've never told you before. It's the story of creation and how we all came to be." This sounded interesting, so I stretched out as far as I could, snuggled my head in her lap, and waited. I'd never given a single thought to how we all came to be. I was a dog, and as far as I knew, I had just always been.

"Billions of years ago, God created the earth. He created the mountains we live in; He created the oceans and the streams; He created the flowers and the trees, the heavens and the skies. Everything we see when we go for our walks or take car trips, God created, and it was all good." *I could vouch for that. Even from my doggie point of view, I could see the beauty of creation.*

"Well, one day God realized He had created this beautiful world, but hadn't created anyone to take care of it for Him or to have a relationship with Him." She stopped and gazed at me lovingly, "The same way I take care of our home, the way we have a relationship and take care of each other, you know?" *Oh, yes, I knew.* She continued, "So, that's when God created the first man and He called him Adam. God gave Adam dominion over the entire earth, which meant, not only would Adam cultivate the earth, but he would also name each and every creature God created on the earth. Those included birds, fish, mammals, everything! Adam loved coming up with names for all of God's creatures. In some cases, he named the whole species then gave each creature a special name. For instance, those things that flew through the sky he called birds, but each kind was beautiful and unique, so he named each kind – robin, sparrow, dove, cardinal, eagle – so many species." *This was very interesting to me because Mom and I had made a summer habit over the years of lying on our backs in the yard, watching the eagles soar overhead. They were majestic and I loved knowing the story of who named them. Back to Mom. The story wasn't over yet.*

"The day came when God brought Adam a very special animal. This animal walked on four legs, had a tail, two ears, two eyes, a nose, and a mouth. It was soft and furry and it barked!"

Wait just one minute! That sounded like me! My ears perked up and I snuggled in closer.

"Adam was drawn to this creature and played with it for days, finding a loyalty in his furry friend not present in any other of God's creatures. They hiked through the Garden of Eden; they swam together in the rivers; they became inseparable. Walking through the Garden one day, Adam found something unusual along the path. Rarely did he ever see a stick lying around because, in its perfection, the Garden's trees never shed their limbs. Thinking maybe God had planted the stick in his path on purpose, Adam picked it up and examined it. Not knowing exactly what to do with it, he nonchalantly tossed it further up the path. To his delight, his furry friend chased it and brought it back to him, laying it at his feet. Just to see what would happen, Adam tossed the stick into the river and watched wide-eyed as his friend jumped right into the water, grabbed the stick between his teeth, and swam straight to the riverbank to once again lay the stick at Adam's feet.

Adam sat down on the riverbank and was surprised when his friend sat right beside him as close as he could get, nuzzling Adam's arm until he wrapped it around him and hugged him tightly. Overcome with affection, Adam kissed his friend on the nose and whispered these words, "What a treasure you are to me, my friend. I never imagined a companion like you. Loyalty is one of your best qualities, but there are so many other qualities that make you special. You live in the moment, not worrying about what happened yesterday or what might happen tomorrow. Do you know what a gift that is? Your unconditional love and faithfulness are unmatched by any other animal I've seen so far. And you're happy all the time. I remember the day I had to leave you alone for hours, not knowing how you'd react when I returned. Were you upset with me for leaving you behind, straying far away from you? No! You were just happy to have me back and greeted me with kisses. Then I think about the time I had to correct you for doing something you shouldn't have. I told you no and reminded you to follow the rules I had taught you. Were you upset? Again, no! You understood the rules were meant to keep you safe and healthy, put in place because I loved you so much. We forgave each other and went on with our day."

Adam and his furry friend sat quietly for a few minutes before he spoke again. "I've given this a lot of thought. Of all the creatures God created and asked me to name, you are the one that most reflects God's qualities: His loyalty, His unconditional love, His ability to meet us exactly where we are at any given time, His faithfulness, and His forgiveness. These five qualities have made naming you much easier than I ever imagined. I know exactly what to call you and I'm sure God will approve. Since you're a reflection of God, the mirror image of the word G-O-D would be D-O-G, so from this day forward, as a reflection of our Creator, you'll be known as DOG!

As Mom ended the story, my doggie heart smiled. I'm not sure exactly how, but somewhere deep inside, I already knew this.

8

Trip to the Beach

We were on our way to the beach! Have you guys ever been to the beach? This was going to be my first time and I was pretty excited. During one of our couch-cuddles, Mom had told me all about the sand and the ocean and the sea creatures we'd find there, but I've gotta tell you, I was having a hard time imagining any of it. All I knew were trees and grass and rocks on our mountain, so the idea of anything else was a mystery to me. I couldn't wait to get there!

I was in the back seat right behind Mom, who was driving the car. She wouldn't allow me to stick my head out the window because she said it was dangerous, but she did put the window halfway down, so my nose could pick up all the scents, and what a sensory overload! The wind smelled so good. I couldn't begin to count the new and interesting smells whizzing by as we drove down the road, heading for a place called Kitty

Hawk on the Outer Banks of North Carolina. Hanging out with Mom has taught me a lot, so let me give you a little background about the Outer Banks.

The Outer Banks is a chain of islands located off the coast of North Carolina. What makes them so special? First, there are a hundred miles of beaches – can you imagine? - and secondly (this was the part Mom loved most), no neon signs, no high-rise hotels, no boardwalks, no tourist traps, just beautiful unspoiled beaches. We were going to be staying in a rental cottage for the weekend and Mom was really looking forward to quiet walks on the beach together. If only she had known...

Okay, let's fast-forward past checking into our cottage, unloading our suitcases, marking a little territory on the bush behind the house, and go straight to stepping onto the beach and seeing the ocean for the first time. W O W!!! Never in my few years of doggie life had I ever seen anything like it! Water, as far as the eye could see. To me, it looked like the biggest water dish on earth. Oh, boy! Oh, boy! Oh, boy! I meant to be a good dog; I really did. I planned to stay right beside Mom and follow the rules, but, c'mon...what's a dog to do in a situation like this? I did the only thing a dog in my position *could* do. I jerked the leash out of Mom's hand and took off! I ran across the sand dunes at top speed, with Mom running as hard as she could behind me, calling my name, *Zen! Zen, stop! Zen, come back!* I heard her, but no way could I stop. I had tunnel

49

vision, which meant all I could see was ocean ahead of me. I don't think I'd ever run this fast in my life. Oh, I ran in the mountains, of course, I did, but this was different – wide open space, so much sky, the wind carrying unbelievable smells straight to my nose, gritty sand under my feet, and endless water up ahead. I was almost there...almost there...almost...THERE! I was there! My feet were wet...now my legs were wet...now my belly...and now – BAM! - a wave broke over top of me, and *all* of me was wet! I came up sputtering! Hey, wait a minute! This water might be wet like the water at home, but it sure didn't taste like the water at home. I realized right away it wasn't meant for drinking; it was meant for playing! Lesson learned!

Suddenly, I felt the tug of the leash and looked around to see Mom's foot on it. She had no choice but to scold me a little. *Zen, don't ever do that again*, she sputtered while trying to catch her breath. *What if we had lost each other? What if something had happened to you?* My safety was her main concern and taking off like that until I was nothing but a tiny speck in the distance had scared her. Honestly? If I had gotten too far away from her and looked around and couldn't find her, I would have been scared, too. Bending down to pick up the leash, she made her point one last time, *Buddy, I love you too much to let anything happen to you, so please, don't ever do that to me again*! I nuzzled her hand to let her know I understood. *Good boy*, she said with a big grin and I knew I was forgiven.

For the rest of our time at the beach, I stayed right with her and believe it or not, it didn't spoil the fun at all. We played in the ocean and had so much fun. At one point, she took me out in the water and actually let me off the leash. I was able to swim a little, catch a wave (that's for any surfers who might be reading my story), and ride it in. Mom called it body surfing. When I hit the beach, I managed to stay put, which took every ounce of control I had. But here's the best part - because I behaved, we were able to do it again and again, and that just goes to show, when you mind your mom, good things happen.

On our second morning in Kitty Hawk, Mom and I got back into the car to travel four miles south to a place called Kill Devil Hills. Back in 1903, two brothers named Orville and Wilbur Wright flew the first powered, controlled airplane off Big Kill Devil Hill. I wasn't sure exactly what flying was unless you counted how fast I ran when we first got to the beach. That sure felt like flying to me! I also wasn't sure what 1903 meant, but according to Mom, 1903 was over a hundred years ago. I might be a dog, but even I know that's a long time! There was no way we could stay in Kitty Hawk, she said, without visiting the scene of the first airplane flight. Humans can fly all over the world, she told me, thanks to the Wright Brothers and what they did right here over a hundred years ago. Even though we couldn't go inside the building because I'm a dog, just seeing this historic spot made her happy and that's all that mattered to me.

So, other than visiting the Wright Brothers' Memorial, the two of us spent all of our time at the beach. Something about the ocean made Mom very zen. Remember why she named me Zen? It meant peaceful, calm, oneness, and that's how the ocean made her feel. She talked about how much she loved the horizon, how free it made her feel to be able to see for miles and miles. She talked about the ocean's power, its vastness. Then she told me something that made my eyes widen. Over 70% of the earth is ocean!! Can you believe that? There was no doubt in my mind I'd never see all of it, but I sure did love the tiny part of the Atlantic Ocean that I *was* seeing.

Which reminds me, have I told you about my close encounter of the crab kind? Nope, I don't think I have. If you've never seen a crab, you can't begin to imagine what funny little creatures they are. They have ten legs, and because they have ten legs, they don't just walk backward and forward; they walk side to side too. Their two front legs are claws and, smart dog that I am, nobody had to tell me I wanted to stay far away from those! Their eyes are on stalks way above their bodies and those eyes can see all the way around. Anyway, I was hanging out on the beach after an exhausting day of body surfing when suddenly I was eyeball to eyeball with this funny-looking sea creature. By now, you guys know me; I'm a friendly, happy-go-lucky kind of fella.

All I wanted to do was say hello, see if maybe this funny little, skittery thing might want to play, so I moved in closer. Whoa! Jump back, Zen, steer clear of those claws. I backed off, but that didn't stop me. My bravery was well-known.

I moved in again, and this time, those front claws came mighty close to my nose. I backed off. I've mentioned before that I'm not a barker, but right now I felt that my big, deep bark might be just the thing to tame the beast, so I barked. Nothing! My bark didn't intimidate the crab at all. It just turned in a circle until it faced Mom and looked at her as if to say, *Human, would you please control your crazy whatever-this-thing-is?* And here's what was really weird – I *thought* I was chasing the crab as we circled each other. I would pounce, the claws would get way too close to my nose, and of course, I'd jump back. No dummy me! But as it ended up, the crab, who was big for a crab, but much smaller than my 65 pounds, was actually chasing me. How did I know that? Well, Mr. Crab was beach-smart. He knew the terrain much better than I did, so every time we circled each other and the claws got too close to my nose, I'd jump backward. Every jump backward put me closer to the water. Before I knew it, we were on the ocean's edge, giving the crab a distinct advantage. After all, this is where he lived. And just when I had given up hope that I'd ever get close enough to make friends with him, he stopped and let me sniff him! But he definitely knew what he was doing because just as my nose almost touched his body, a huge wave crashed over us and the crab disappeared. I looked around. *What happened? Where did he go?* Turning in circles, I barked at the waves. *Okay, ocean, give him up! We were this close to becoming friends.* I searched and searched, scanned the shore with my excellent vision, but I couldn't see the crab. I guess it was time to give up, but just to be on the safe side, I looked around one more time. Nope, I couldn't see him. I sighed a big, deep sigh.

Do you want to know what else I couldn't see? I couldn't see the two crab eyes just above the water's surface that watched me as I finally gave up and walked away.

9

CAMP COULBOURNE AND COLIN

Sometimes my mom had to travel, and the sad thing about that was there were times she couldn't take me with her. You see, Mom is an author, and here's the thing about authors – sometimes they have to go on the road for book signings or personal appearances, and on those occasions, she had to leave me behind. This broke our hearts, but there was no other choice. Leave it to Mom to find a way to brighten my world when she had to be away from me. I'm guessing all of you have either grandparents, aunts and uncles, or close friends of your parents who babysit when you need a sitter. Am I right? Well, I needed a sitter and Mom had just the couple – her close friends Pam and Giff, who had a house nestled in the woods not far away from us.

Whenever Mom had to be away, whether it was for days or just one night, she'd arrange for me to stay with 'Uncle' Giff and 'Aunt' Pam at what we lovingly referred to as Camp Coulbourne. As much as I missed Mom when she traveled and as happy as I was to see her when she got back, I had a great time there. Giff and I would hang together outside all day long. Sometimes we'd play, sometimes he and Pam would work in their yard while I kept myself busy marking this new territory and sometimes, I would just lie on the deck, soaking up the sun. By the time we went inside for the evening, a full day of running around in the fresh mountain air and sunshine had made me dog-tired. That's when Pam came to the rescue with her homemade dog treats. Not store-bought, but *homemade* and, boy, were they scrumptious! Maybe I'll include a couple of her recipes at the end of this book.

My favorite time at Camp Coulbourne was when their little grandson, Kinsey, came to visit. He was only two years old and not much taller than I was, which might be the reason we had so much fun together. It wasn't often I got to play with a human who was just my size, and my natural instincts told me to be gentle with him and to watch out for him. After all, he was just a little guy. Kinsey loved to talk to me. I can't say I understood every single word he said because he was just learning to talk, but he told me great stories that went on for minutes and were punctuated by giggles and laughter. On our walks together, I would adjust my stride to make sure we stayed side by side. If you could have seen us, you'd have known for sure that in those moments, Kinsey and I were the best of friends.

Speaking of best buds...after my success at the nursing home, Mom and I looked for opportunities for me to make a difference in people's lives. I don't think I've mentioned that she owned two houses on top of the mountain. We lived in one of them and her son Colin lived in the other. Colin had something called autism and Mom explained to me what that meant. First, he lived with full-time care, meaning someone had to be with him at all times. Secondly, he was nonverbal, which meant he couldn't talk. Can you imagine not being able to say what you want to say *when* you want to say it? Can you imagine not being able to tell your parents you love them? That's how it was for Colin, so he had to find ways to let his caregivers know what he needed. Sometimes this came in the form of meltdowns during which he would cry and even scream in his frustration to get his point across.

Enter...ME!

Mom took me over to see Colin one day. I walked in expecting a huge smile of welcome, but that wasn't what happened. Colin ignored me like I wasn't even there. I couldn't believe it! I don't think I had ever been ignored since the day I was rescued by Mom. To tell you the truth, I didn't know exactly what to do, but Mom's look told me to stay the course, so I did. We continued going to Colin's every few days, with me determined to make him like me. Heck, not even like me, but to pay some kind of attention to me. Have you ever had a situation like that? Maybe you've been the new kid in class and all the other kids had their friends already and you felt kind of shy and left out? But then one day, someone finally walks over and smiles at you, and suddenly you know everything will be okay. That's how I felt, very left out, until the day we had a breakthrough.

Every day we spent at Colin's saw me being my most charming self. I smiled; I pranced; I nuzzled. Mom would give me the signal to speak and I would speak, long and hard. Nothing! Then one day, Colin started working himself into a meltdown. I had seen it before and, honestly, it wasn't fun. This particular time Colin was sitting on the floor, smacking the floor with his hands and yelling really loud. And if it was loud for a human, you can imagine how loud it was to me. Hesitantly, I walked toward him, taking great care to stay away from the hands that were smacking the floor. The best approach, I thought to myself, would be to stay behind him, so I did. I touched his back with my nose, but he didn't seem to notice. Mom sat on the floor across from Colin, talking soothingly to him. He let her hold one of his hands just for a minute, but that minute was long enough for me to sneak in, lie down next to him and lay my head on his leg. I was a tiny bit nervous because, in these situations, Colin could be unpredictable. But Mom and I made a great team. Between the two of us, we managed to calm him down. I pressed my warm body into his side and managed to keep my breaths deep and slow, which Colin picked up on. His breathing slowed down, the yelling stopped, and for the first time ever, he reached over and lay his hand on my back. He wasn't really petting me like other humans did, but at least he was paying attention to me. After months of trying unsuccessfully to be his friend, I finally felt we had made progress.

Such a difference between Kinsey and Colin, but let me tell you, both friendships are valuable to me. Colin was different, true, but I've learned so much from him. Kids, even when we're different, we have many things in common. We all want to be loved. We all want to feel safe. We all want to know we matter to the people we love. That's even true of dogs. So, my best advice to you is this. Feel gratitude that all your parts work, that you can walk and talk, run and play. And, if you meet someone who can't do those things or is different from you in some other way, be patient and take the time to get to know them, to include them, to make them feel special. When you do that, not only will you learn valuable lessons from them, but you'll realize God created each and every one of us, and to Him, we are each a masterpiece to be treasured and loved no matter how different we might be.

10

LOCKDOWN

Mom was watching the news on TV. I was snoozing right beside her, not the least bit concerned about what the news was saying. Look, I'm a dog! When that TV thing is on, people on the screen talk constantly, and if I paid attention to everything they said, I'd never get my beauty sleep. I was content to lie by her side, getting the occasional belly rub or kiss on top of my head. But all of the lovey stuff came to a halt when Mom jumped up, saying, "I don't believe this! How could this be happening?" I wanted to try to answer, but I had no idea what she was talking about.

She started toward the kitchen and I hopped up to follow her. I watched her as she opened and closed almost every cupboard door we had, looking for... who knows what. I had no idea. "This is unbelievable," she said with a worried look on her face. "I don't have any anti-bacterial wipes or sprays. We're low on paper towels and toilet paper. As a matter of fact, we need groceries, period. You need your dog food, Zen, and I'm almost totally out of treats." *Now wait just one minute! No treats for me! That wasn't an option!* "Okay, okay...they're saying we have to wear masks when we go out. They're saying we have to stay at least 6 feet apart." *What was going on? No way did I want to stay 6 feet away from Mom. Not ever!* Then glancing over at me, she corrected herself, "That doesn't mean the two of us, buddy. No one can make me stay 6 feet away from you. They're talking about humans." *Whew! Good to know, but I wished she would tell me what was going on.*

We went back to the family room, where our little family of two settled in once again in front of the television. I tried to pay attention this time, but they were saying words I had never heard before – pandemic, coronavirus, social distancing, something about flattening some kind of curve. Mom pulled me close and started to explain. "Zen, for the first time in my lifetime, the whole world is experiencing a pandemic, which means there's a virus out there that can make humans sick. They're telling us to take precautions by wearing masks and staying away from each other. And they're saying we should plan to be locked down for two weeks, which means I need to make a trip to the grocery store to load up on everything." I licked her hand. "Don't worry, buddy, it's you and me against the world, right? We'll get through this together. As long as we have each other, we'll be fine." She held me close and even though she tried to hide them, I saw the tears glistening in her eyes. "We'll be okay, my Zen."

And that was the beginning of a lockdown that ended up lasting a year, maybe more. If you were alive in 2020, you know exactly what I'm talking about because your family went through it too. It wasn't all bad, was it? Families spent more time together. Life slowed down. As for me, I have to admit; I kinda liked it! Mom was with me all the time. She didn't have to travel because everything was canceled – no book signings or appearances of any kind. Just Mom and me hanging out day after day, watching movies, eating comfort food, and going for walks on top of our mountain, which was okay under the new guidelines because we rarely saw any people. Besides, breathing in the fresh air and getting our Vitamin D from the sunshine was good for both of us.

During the summer of lockdown, we'd go over to visit Colin, staying on his front deck and six feet away from him. Mom would wear her mask or a face shield to make sure he was protected. Sometimes we'd go back to our house, she'd turn on the sprinkler, and we'd take turns running through it. Getting wet on a hot summer's day felt fantastic. It was a little like having a bath, but better because I could run free.

My favorite season in lockdown, or at any time if you want to know the truth, was winter. Being half Husky meant I was bred for the snow. I was also bred to run long distances with minimal food, a trait that came from my sled-pulling ancestors. Put those two things together and you can see why I loved winter so much. I loved it much more than Mom did, but she was a trooper, layering up to go outside with me in the frigid temperatures at least four times a day. Playing in the snow was my thing! No matter how high it was, I could plow through the snow at top speed. One of my favorite things was running as fast as I could, then diving into a fresh snowbank and coming out with the white stuff all over my face. That always made Mom laugh really hard, so I'd do it over and over again until we both needed to go inside to warm up.

Mom was genius at coming up with games for us to play during the lockdown. One was called food scattering. She would take my kibble, scatter some on the floor, and I would eat it bit by bit. Since there was really no challenge in scattering food that way, she decided to take small amounts and hide them around the house, forcing me to sniff them out before I could eat them. This, she told me, was basic scent work and the reward for me at the end was the satisfaction of finding the food and eating it. Did you know that licking and chewing are very relaxing to a dog? See? Mom rarely did anything without knowing it would be good for me.

Of course, during lockdown, we played normal games like tug-of-war and fetch, but I definitely had one game I loved more than all the others. Mom called it the Toilet Paper Challenge and until we were stuck

in the house for months on end, we had never played it. Yep, that was another good thing about lockdown because this game was the best! Here's what she would do. In our long back hallway, she would place toilet paper rolls on the floor, side by side from wall to wall. When she was done, she'd give me the signal, and I'd run down the hallway and jump over the row of toilet paper. When I cleared the first row, she added a second row on top of the first. When I jumped two rows, she added a third, and when I made it over the third...well, you know. So, I kept jumping and she kept adding toilet paper until she didn't have any left. When she ran out, she used rolls of paper towels on top of the toilet paper rolls. One paper towel roll was equal to three toilet paper rolls stacked on top of each other, which made this much more challenging, but I kept jumping...three rows...four rows...five rows...could this be any more fun? I cleared seven rows and went back down the hall to try for eight. Okay, eight was looking pretty high. Not sure I could do it. I took a moment to compose myself and then off I went. The best thing about toilet paper rolls and paper towel rolls in an empty hallway? You can miss the jump, plow right through the middle and not hurt yourself or break one single thing!

The months in lockdown ended up being as much fun as we could make them. Our creativity flourished and our love deepened. And, like I said earlier, having Mom with me every minute of every day was my dream come true.

11

THE RAINBOW BRIDGE

Mom and I were close from the day we met, but we became even closer during lockdown. I didn't think I could love her more, but I found out I could, and my dog love was unconditional. I didn't care if Mom was rich or poor; I didn't care how big her car was. When she gained a few pounds, she was still beautiful to me. And if she stayed in her jammies all day, which happened a lot during lockdown, it was a-okay with me as long as she was there. The best day of my life was the day I adopted my human.

We were cuddled up on the sofa having couch-cuddle time when Mom told me there was something she wanted to talk to me about. "Zen," she said to me, "do you know how much richer my life is because of you?" *Of course, I did and that worked both ways.* "Of all the animals I've had over the years, and mind you, I've loved every single one of them, you're the one that changed everything for me." My ears stood straight up. *If what she said was true, then I knew for certain I'd been doing my job.* "You've been my trusted companion. Eight years ago, you walked into my life and took away all my loneliness. You've cheered me up when I felt sad." She took my face in her hands and kissed my nose. "I mean, how could I ever feel sad or lonely when I look at this face?" *I softened my big brown eyes and looked at her with all the love I could muster.* "You've been right beside me when I've been sick and I've been right there for you whenever you've needed me. You, my friend, are the love-of-my-life dog. In my wildest dreams, I never imagined having a dog so perfect for me. I've always been convinced God knew how badly we needed each other. I'm totally convinced He sent me to the football game that Friday night because He knew we would take one look at each other and fall in love. He knew. And I give thanks to Him every day for the gift of you." *Me too! God had looked out for me too!*

"So, here's what I want to talk to you about. We're both getting older and can't do the things we once did as easily as we once did them, right?" *Boy, was Mom right! I used to hop up into the car with no problem, but lately, it's been a little more of a challenge. Sometimes I can do it and sometimes I can't.* "As we get older, things change, we slow down, we don't have the energy we once had, and that can be frustrating. But it's all part of life, all very normal. *I'm not sure I liked this normal all that much, but I was willing to hear her out.*

"Our lives on earth don't last forever and even though that might sound sad, it really isn't." *What?!? I might not be here forever??* "Do you want to know why it isn't a sad thing?" *I 'talked,' trying to say the word yes!* "Because when we leave this earth, we'll go to a place where we *will* live forever." *Whew! That sounded hopeful. What was this place called and where was it located exactly?* "That place is called Heaven and both of us will go there someday. However, we might not go there at the same time." *I fidgeted on the sofa. No way did I want to go anywhere without my mom.* "I know, I know." She stroked me gently. "We've been a team for so many years it's almost impossible to imagine doing anything separate from one another, but we can and when it becomes necessary, we will. When the time comes, we'll do what we have to do, knowing that one

day we'll be together forever in a place so beautiful we can't begin to envision it."

I had never been a whiner, but I couldn't stop myself from whining just a little.

"No, no, no, buddy, don't feel sad." She turned to face me on the sofa.

"Let's imagine that you go to this beautiful place before I do. What will you find while you wait for me?" She got a dreamy look in her eyes. "First, you'll be young and spry like you used to be. No more struggling to jump up or down, no more struggling at all. You'll be able to run full speed, nonstop for hours. And, oh, the places you'll have to run - endless meadows; not only endless, but flawless. The temperature will be perfect, so you'll never be too hot or too cold. Remember months ago, when you had a tummy problem and had to go to the vet?" *Oh, yeah, I remembered. As hard as I tried, I didn't make it to the edge of the woods that time!* "Well, no more tummy problems, no more vet visits, just perfect health forever and ever!" *Okay, the perfect health thing sounded good to me!* "You'll have all the food you need, all the water you need and more friends to play with than you've ever had in your life! You'll even meet the dogs I rescued before you came into my life." *Oh, wow, that meant I'd meet Sophie and Gracie, Thika, and Pippin! I liked the sound of that! Even so, I couldn't stop the whine that escaped me. But I'd miss my mom!!*

"Zen, I know what you're thinking...but what about me? You'll have everything in this glorious place except me, your best friend, right?" *Exactly, precisely, nail on the head!* "Well, my friend, here's the good part. When you get there, you'll wait for me, but while you're waiting, you'll have so many friends and be so busy running, jumping, playing, and exploring you won't really think of me every single second." *That, I couldn't imagine, hard as I tried. Mom was everything to me.* "And here's what will happen one day when you least expect it. You'll be with a group of your friends. Maybe you'll be busy sniffing the beautiful flowers, or maybe you'll be sniffing out the deer you'll finally be able to play with." *The deer would be there?? That was something a guy could look forward to.* "Suddenly, you'll pick up a scent – not the deer or the flowers, but a scent you remember from long ago. You'll stop short as memories come flooding back – memories of car trips and couch cuddles; memories of loving and being loved; memories of shopping and banking, of Colin and Miss Ruby." *My doggie heart was pounding, waiting to hear what would happen next.*

"You'll lift your head and with those keen eyes of yours, look far into the distance. Remember, your vision will be perfect! The scent will grow stronger and suddenly, you'll know exactly who the scent belongs to. Your tail will wag like it's never wagged before. Your body will begin to quiver all over." *Just the way it had quivered eight years before when I was in a crate in*

72

the back of a truck, heading for my new home on top of the mountain. That's when I picked up the scent... Mom's scent! "In the distance, you'll spot me. Without hesitation, you'll leave your friends behind, running across the meadow as fast as your legs will carry you. And then...there I'll be, right in front of you, waiting with my arms wide open. We'll tumble to the ground together, roll in the grass together, howl, and laugh in joyous celebration. And this time, you'll be my guide, showing me everything you discovered while you waited for me. We'll explore every inch of it together. The memory of all the years we were apart will melt away. And that, my handsome Zen, is when we'll walk side by side and cross the Rainbow Bridge together, never to be parted again."

Epilogue

I was having so much fun running up and down the grassy, green hills, chasing my tail, and falling over in a heap when I couldn't catch it. Between tail chases, my friends and I had this great game going - one of us would stand still, and the others would take a long, fast run and leap over him. *Hmm, that rang a distant bell in my memory, but I couldn't quite bring it to the surface.* My friends and I took really good care of each other. We shared everything. We swam in the river together, climbed the mountains together, raced each other, and had unbelievable games of fetch and tug-o-war. Every few days, a man named Adam would visit with us, playing with us for hours on end. We could tell he loved us as much as we loved him. I gotta tell ya, though, the first time I met him, a strange feeling washed over me. *Adam. ADAM! Why did his name feel so familiar?* But, hey, I was a dog and easily distracted by the next shiny thing, so even though the question entered my head, I was able to let it go and get right back to playing.

It was a gorgeous day, perfect, really. The temperature was perfect. The blue sky was perfect. I felt stronger and healthier than I had in a long time, which meant I was perfect. My friends were perfect too. All of us with energy to spare. We could run and jump all day and never get tired, but when it came time to sleep...well, we were perfect sleepers, lying on the soft ground all cuddled up, keeping each other company— cuddling...*why did the feel of warm bodies next to mine jog something in my memory?* I shook it off because today we weren't sleeping; we were scattered all over the meadow, playing a game we made up called 'who can hide in plain sight'. Whoever was IT had to find all the rest of us, and to make this more challenging, we had to find a spot where we would blend in with our surroundings, lying close to the ground, barely moving a muscle. I was lying in front of a white hydrangea tree. Some of the branches were close to the ground, so I figured since I was almost all white, maybe I would blend in. With my nose on the ground, I opened one eye to try to peek around and see what my buddy Scout was up to. He was doing exactly what his name suggested, scouting around trying to find us. By my count, he had found four of us already. And he was getting closer to my hiding spot, so I closed my eyes and tried to make myself disappear.

Uh-oh, my tail wanted to wag. *No, stop! No wagging!!* But it had a mind of its own. I had to use every ounce of concentration I had to try to keep my tail still and close to the ground. *Wait! What was going on with my nose? It was twitching!* Thank goodness a twitching nose wasn't as noticeable as a wagging tail. Or was it? Then the worst possible thing happened. My entire body started quivering! *What was going on?!?* How could I possibly blend in when I was quivering all over? Then I smelled it. A familiar scent. *How?... Was it possible?...Was my nose deceiving me?* I lifted my head, not caring if Scout noticed me or not. This was much more important than winning the 'who can hide

in plain sight' game. This was my past entering into my present. At least that's what it felt like.

I lifted my head to get a good look around. *In the distance...what* **was** *that way off in the distance?* I stood up. Everything around me faded as memories bombarded me at warp speed...car rides...the edge of the woods...peeing on a Christmas tree...my personal appearances at the bank...being outsmarted by a crab at the beach...being held and loved when I was sick... living on the top of the mountain...our big, beautiful house...being a radio star...lockdown...the first time I smelled this scent I was sitting in a crate at a high school football game. The scent I knew I'd never forget. The scent that belonged to my best friend. The scent that long ago told me I would be loved and safe forever. THAT scent! The scent of the angel who rescued me! And now she was an angel for real?

I took off running! I don't think I've ever run so fast in my life! I covered the distance between us in no time flat. And there she was, right in front of me, smiling her 100-megawatt smile, arms wide open, inviting me in. I barreled into her, knocking us both over. I didn't think the hugs and kisses would ever stop. We rolled in the grass, laughing and squealing. Then we lay quietly while she told me how much she had missed me and how elated she was to be with me again. I covered her face in kisses, hoping she understood I felt the exact same way. "Zen, love-of-my-life, when I knew I'd be coming here, I had one prayer. Please let the first thing I see be my beautiful boy running toward me as fast as he did on earth, and my prayer was answered. Except here in this heavenly place, I think you were even faster." She winked.

We stood up and I showed her around. I even introduced her to my new friends, a few of whom she had loved on earth before she met me. "Sophie, Gracie," she called out in delight. Mom and the girls made a huge fuss over each other before I was finally able to lead her across the meadow to the bridge, with Sophie and Gracie close behind. Reading my mind, she answered my unasked question. "Yes," she assured me, "I remember our long talk about the Rainbow Bridge. It's stunning, even more beautiful than I imagined it or could ever have described it to you." We stared at each other for a long time. "Thank you for waiting for me, my Zen." Then, cupping my head in her hands, she looked at me with all the love she had stored up since the last time we were together. "Are we ready?" she asked. We both looked at Sophie and Gracie, who got in line right behind me. Yes, we were. With joy in our hearts and no hesitation at all, we crossed the Rainbow Bridge and walked into eternity together.

Zen's Favorite Homemade Treats

Pumpkin Butter Treats

- 2 cups flour
- 1 cup canned pumpkin
- ½ cup smooth peanut butter (xylitol-free)

Preheat oven to 375. Mix peanut butter and pumpkin together, stir in flour and combine into a dough. Roll dough out on floured surface to either ¼" or ½ ". Cut out treats with a dog bone cutter or any small cookie cutter, place on ungreased cookie sheet or you can use parchment paper. Bake for 12 minutes or until light brown.

Peanut Parmesan Surprise

- 2 Cups whole wheat flour
- 1 Cup smooth peanut butter (xylitol-free)
- ¼ Cup oats
- 1 Cup chicken broth
- 1 Tablespoon baking powder
- Parmesan cheese

Preheat oven to 375. Mix flour , oats and baking powder together. Add peanut butter and chicken broth. Knead dough (like pizza dough)) about 2 to 3 minutes. Roll out to about ¼ " to ½ ", cut with a dog bone cutter or any small cookie cutter. Sprinkle just a small amount of parmesan cheese on top. Bake on a parchment paper lined cookie sheet for 25 minutes or until light brown. Store in refrigerator for 20 days or freeze.